"...Very Funny! This book will hit home with a lot of mothers (and not just mothers of twins or triplets!)"

-Dr. Burton Rochelson, Chief of Obstetrics, NSUH

"As with Lori's first book, I started laughing the minute I started reading. Anyone going through these experiences will be nodding their heads off in agreement."

-Bianca S., mother of twin boys, Tampa Bay, Florida

"A hilarious (and totally true) romp through the trials and tribulations of pregnancy & early parenthood."

-Dr. Loren Yellin, Assistant Clinical Professor of Pediatrics, Albert Einstein College of Medicine

"As a mother of twins, I could relate to every chapter. A must read!"

-Leigh Kamraoui, Mèze, Occitanie, France

"...Strangers asking really personal questions? No help from family? Totally relatable. I strongly recommend this book to anyone parenting multiples who needs a good laugh."

-Marla V. -mom to boy/girl twins, S. New Jersey

LAUGHING *IS* CONCEIVABLE NO MATTER
HOW MANY YOU'RE CARRYING

Other Books by the Author

Laughing *IS* Conceivable: One Woman's Extremely Funny Peek into the Extremely Unfunny World of Infertility*

Laughing *IS* Conceivable: From End of School to Back-to-School (I love my kids. I love my kids. I *LOVE* MY KIDS!)

*Spanish Version- La Risa *ES* Concebible: Una Mirada Extremadamente Graciosa de Una Mujer, al Mundo Extremadamente No Gracioso de la Infertilidad

LAUGHING *IS* CONCEIVABLE NO MATTER HOW MANY YOU'RE CARRYING:

Insanity in its Infancy

by Lori Shandle-Fox

LAF Publications

copyright © 2018 by Lori Shandle-Fox

No part of this publication may be reproduced in any material form (including photo-copying or storing in any medium by electronic means and whether or not transiently or incidentally to some other use of this publication) without the written permission of the copyright holder except in accordance with provisions of the Copyright, Designs and Patents Act 1988.

ISBN   978-0-9600779-0-8   (paperback)

Cover Designs:

Sandy Vazan Illustration

Cover Photo:

Jane Bonin at Covershot Classics Photography

Cover Model:

Kellie McLeod

I dedicate this book:

To my husband Lloyd, my kids, Jacob, Carly, and Hayley and my sister, Joni. But for them, I would have no material.

To my parents, Jerome (Jerry) Shandle and Harriet Shandle who saw first-hand the dangers of what happens when people with very different senses of humor reproduce.

To my wonderful friends Roberta Saltzman and Sharon Sevransky who have, quite frankly, saved my ass on more than one occasion. (And I'm hoping this dedication will give them enough incentive to continue to do so whenever necessary.)

To Nicole and Theresa who worked at BPCC and all of the other strangers who voluntarily helped us when those who knew us wouldn't, couldn't, or shouldn't.

And to you:

Whether you're pregnant with one baby or just had twins or your brother-in-law has triplets or you have a bunch of small kids close in age... Whatever brought you here, you belong. And I truly appreciate you coming along for this little jaunt through my buffoonery.

Table of Contents

Acknowledgements..xi

Introduction...xiii

Chapter One: Getting Pregnant with More than One Baby aka How I Got Myself Into This........1

    A. "Waiting for Mr. Right…and Waiting…and Waiting. So what's the hold-up? Is he stuck in traffic or what?"

    B. "Who Needs Medical Intervention When You Have Divine Intervention?"

    C. "If It's Meant to Happen…" Oh screw you.

    D. "We Wanted that You Should Be Pregnant… But Not *So* Pregnant."

    E. "In Case You've Ever Wondered What the Opposite of 'Random Acts of Kindness' Was"

    F. "I Was an Infertegnant. It's sort of like a turducken."

Chapter Two: Staying Pregnant with More than One Baby..21

A. "Dr. Doom"

B. "And I Was County Cork"

C. "My Ultra Ultrasounds: When the Bill Comes, My Insurance Company Gets Up from the Table and Hides in the Bathroom"

D. "My Ultra Ultrasounds: Turn Left at the Ear. You Have Arrived at Your Destination."

E. "The Return of Dr. Doom"

F. "Your Typical, Run-of-the-Mill Pregnancy Annoyances: You Name It, It Annoyed Me."

G. "Dr. Doom's Words Still Loomed. But How Many of Her Predictions Actually Came True?"

Chapter Three: Giving Birth to More than One Baby..65

A. "Re-enacting the Stateroom Scene from *A Night at the Opera*: My Hospital (1/3 of a) Room"

B. "Re-enacting the Stateroom Scene from *A Night at the Opera* Part II: The Deliverance"

C. "Tiptoeing Through Medical Minefields"

D. "My Husband Teaches Me My ABCs"

E. "My First Eviction Notice"

F. "Eviction Day"

Chapter Four: Taking Care of More than One Baby aka Getting from the NICU to Nick Jr....93

A. "Re-enacting the Stateroom Scene from *A Night at the Opera* Part III: The Pediatrician's Office"

B. "Help is on the Way...Not to *Us*... Maybe to a Tornado or Something"

C. "'3 Against 2' Starts to Look Pretty Good"

D. "Sight-Seeing in NYC is Lots of Fun...And What a Sight We Were"

E. "Heading South in More Ways than One- A Post-Infantry Roundup"

Afterword: The Fox Kids: Where Are They Now? How should I know? They're probably around here somewhere……………………......................115

Come Learn from My Confusion: Questions that Still Stump Me…………...119

Come Learn from My Blunders: My Final Two Cents to Parents of Many Babies…Or Even Just One…………………………………………...................123

About the Author………………………......................128

Acknowledgements

Thanks to all of the high-risk maternal-fetal doctors, nurses and staffs who are so dedicated to the health and well-being of our babies not to mention their irritable, hormoned-up, nervous wreck mothers. I especially want to thank all of those at North Shore. Here's hoping that I'm not personally responsible for any of you re-thinking your career path or seeking early retirement at thirty-five.

Laughing *IS* Conceivable No Matter How Many You're Carrying

Introduction

I'll tell you right now: This little book isn't about the joys of motherhood and "Aw, look at her with the cereal box on her head!" It's easy to laugh at the adorable antics of babies: The things we love to post and share. It's harder to laugh at what it's *really* like to get pregnant, be pregnant, give birth, and take care of a baby day in and day out. And even harder when it's more than one baby. So if you're having a nightmare of a pregnancy or struggling (even suffering) with an infant or twins or triplets or a bunch of little kids who are very close in age... Honey, I'm here to tell you: **Not only aren't you alone, you're not even in the minority**.

And that friend of your cousin's friend or that woman in that online support group who loved every moment of her pregnancy and was sad to see it go and whose newborn quadruplets are always fed and clean and sleep when they're supposed to and now she's posting from Oahu and "the quads" in their sunglasses are "so cute!" while she's training for a marathon and getting her master's degree in Greek literature and you feel like such a failure and there must be something wrong with you because you don't even have time to go to the toilet let alone Oahu and where would you get the money to travel anyway? And and... Look... *Nobody* with four, two, or a single newborn has a stress-free life. Some handle it better, have more help, more money, true. But that carefree woman with her online bullshit at the luau...That's all it is...bullshit. A fairytale. A faux perfect life devised to make all of us who know her green as her grass skirt with envy. I avoid her as much as possible. And when I can't, I imagine all of her stories, comments, and online photo shoots starting with: "Once upon a time..." May I recommend you do the same?

Now come. Let the rest of us real parents with real lives who really love our kids all laugh together in spite of the hardships of our clumsy pregnancies and chaotic homes... and in the face of them.

Laughing *IS* Conceivable No Matter How Many You're Carrying

Chapter One: Getting Pregnant with More than One Baby aka How I Got Myself Into This

Even if you haven't read my first book, *Laughing IS Conceivable: One Woman's Extremely Funny Peek into the Extremely Unfunny World of Infertility*, you just read my summary-length title which I'm thinking is enough of a hint as to how I got myself into this whole "multiple babies" situation. And *this* is how I got myself into the situation that got me into *that* situation.

A. Waiting for Mr. Right... and Waiting... and Waiting... So what's the holdup? Is he stuck in traffic or what?

My wedding, actually the engagement, actually the actual dating is when the lunacy began. If my husband-to-be and I had been younger, that common remark: "Let's get married and start a family" might have been a two-part undertaking. We'll get married and then, at some later date, down the road apiece, over yonder, start a family like a normal couple. But since we were both in our extremely late thirties when we met and neither of us had ever been married or had kids, we went from speed dating to speed mating. It was about as romantic as it sounds.

"Hi I'm Lori."

"Hi I'm Lloyd."

"Our names sound cute together and you smell nice. We should get married. If you don't mind me asking: How old are you?"

"I'll be thirty-nine in two months."

"*I'll* be thirty-nine in two months!"

"Wow, that's another cute thing to tell our kids!"

"Do you want kids?"

"I do!"

"Congratulations! I now pronounce you husband and wife."

"Speaking of kids...uh oh look at the time on my biological clock... Half past thirty-nine. We'd better go. The rest of you can stay. The band is booked for another hour."

After having waited so long to find the right person, I would have liked to have been a fiancée for more than twenty minutes. The only problem is that when you're older, so tend to be everyone and everything around you. Families, both the ones we already had and the one we hoped to create, played a large part in the decision to set our plans on warp speed. Had we waited even another year or two to get married, who knows how many elderly relatives--or potential children--we would have had left? We weighed the pros and cons of waiting.

"On the negative side, we might not have some of our family at the wedding. On the positive side, we might not have some…of...hmm. It sure would un-complicate the seating chart. And we could probably save a few bucks by lopping a whole tier off the cake."

But waiting was too much of a crapshoot. Who really knew how many good eggs I had left or how long our relatives would linger?

Our plan was simple: We were going to get married and start a family all in the same day.

After all, *everyone* gets pregnant on their wedding night, right?

Boy was I going to be productive that day. I was going to dance with all four of my new sisters-in-law and create their future niece or nephew all in a three hour span. Following the reception and conception, Lloyd and I would celebrate in the bridal suite / baby moon Jacuzzi (after I cleared it with my OB/GYN, of course) from which I would order everything non-alcoholic on the room service menu because, after all, I was eating for two, right? Maybe I could even speed up the pregnancy and have a water birth since I would already be in the tub and check-out wasn't until noon.

Well, I didn't get pregnant on my wedding night…and still wasn't pregnant on the night of our first anniversary.

B. Who Needs Medical Intervention When You Have Divine Intervention?

During our brief engagement, Lloyd and I met a monsignor at a barbecue who blessed us, finishing with:

"Usually when I bless couples they end up having twins."

Wait, what? I don't know much about Catholic prayers but isn't "Amen" Latin for "The End"? What's with this "Oh by the way" he just tossed in there? You're allowed to add asterisks to prayers? My first thought was:

"Oh geez, how do you undo a blessing? Isn't that like trying to squeeze eye drops out of your pupils?"

If I'd known then how excruciatingly complicated, exhausting, and expensive the next year of my life would be, I might have taken the monsignor's generous no-hassle twin set offer more seriously instead of gambling on what was behind Door #3. That's the last time I ever try to undo a blessing.

Month after month after month I tried to get pregnant. Too impatient to wait for my barbecue monsignor's blessing to kick in, I begrudgingly called a fertility clinic and stated my case to the receptionist. As she was confirming my appointment in three weeks, a man suddenly grabbed the phone.

"This is Dr. Martin. You're almost forty-one and you've been trying to get pregnant for a year? That's long enough. See you tomorrow at ten."

As I hung up, I mumbled to myself:

"Wow, the doctor made the appointment himself. That's bad. He heard your age and thought: 'Three weeks for an appointment?! This bitch doesn't even have time to waste talking to the receptionist.'"

C. "If It's Meant to Happen..." Oh screw you.

At that first appointment, the reproductive endocrinologist / appointment secretary asked Lloyd and me a million questions about our health histories and those of our immediate relatives, our semi-immediate relatives, and our "I couldn't pick her out of a three-person line-up" relatives.

"Has anyone in your family ever had multiple sclerosis? Muscular dystrophy? Carpal tunnel syndrome?"

"What about Parkinson's disease? Lou Gehrig's disease? Tommy John surgery?"

"Have you or your partner or your mother-in-law's nephew on her father's side ever had or had sexual contact with anyone who has ever had sexual contact with a man who has taken money for sexual contact with another man in Nigeria or the Isle of Man, even once, in the last eight years?"

And I'm like: "I I don't know. I should have asked at the wedding."

I was then poked, prodded, and probed with

hoses, needles, and various household appliances. I even had the privilege of holding my urine for several hours while they shot dye into my hole like it was the clown's mouth at the carnival. (If my bladder had popped would I have won a non-descript crunchy stuffed animal? Is it a bear or a dog?)

Meanwhile, Lloyd's "ordeal" involved an intimate cup and gown ceremony with a Victoria's Secret catalogue. After that, as I underwent a year of unspeakable things both at home and on the examination table, Lloyd faced his biggest challenge in the waiting room: Seeing the Wi-Fi password without getting up.

I was unofficially diagnosed with OBS: "Old Bitty Syndrome". There was no explanation of why I couldn't get pregnant other than my age or more precisely, the age of my eggs.

The first course of action for us was intrauterine insemination (IUI). It's basically lab sex. They put his in yours without yours actually touching his. I got that definition from a medical journal. (Why are you looking for a footnote? Don't you trust me?) When four rounds of that failed, we moved on to in vitro fertilization (IVF) where the woman's eggs and the man's sperm are put together in a cozy place in hopes that a few of them will make nice-nice. (Millions of children have been created this way as was, I believe, the premise for *The Bachelor in Paradise*.) Due to my advanced age, they put four resulting embryos back in me-- which is a lot. None of them took. Then they tried the next best ones which had been frozen. Those became my children. And at moments of supreme frustration when my twelve year olds are rolling around the floor kicking, screaming, smacking and scratching, I've been known to turn to Lloyd and say:

"This is what you get when you use the back-up batch. It's like buying generic mayonnaise."

D. We Wanted That You Should Be Pregnant…But Not *So* Pregnant

There was a suspicion that I was having "more than one" after my first post-frozen embryo transfer (FET) blood test. The HCG hormone level for a viable pregnancy is around 50. Mine was 289.

Moments after a triplet pregnancy was confirmed via ultrasound a few weeks later, I suddenly realized that I was the only one in the examination room who was speaking... or breathing. I called through my stirruped feet:

"Honey? Doctor? Honey? Doctor? Could someone please acknowledge the half-naked woman lying on the table? You're killing my self-esteem here."

I sat up on my elbows. Lloyd and the doctor had the same look on their faces: Like the about-to-be victim in a horror movie who sees their attacker coming a half-second too late-- accompanied, I'm sure, by the same panicked thought:

"Aw shit! How did *this* happen?!"

Then each's mind went off on its own tangent: My husband Lloyd was thinking: "Triplets?! Stroller x3, car seat x3, mini-van x3 (???), crib x3, swing x3, bibs x3, formula x3, diapers x3, high chair x3, spoons x3, clothes x3, ratty toy they-insist-on-carrying-with-them-everywhere x3, Happy Meals x3, carnival rides x3, karate classes x3, dance classes x3, hot yoga classes x3, color index cards that will be on every school supplies list but never once used x3, pens x3, paper x3, pediatrician x3, summer camp x3, braces x3, iPhone x3, technology that hasn't even been invented yet x3, "Here, don't tell Mommy" bribes x3, bar/bas-mitzvahs x3, dermatologist x3, 20 year old car with 200,000 miles on it x3, college x3, college transferred to x3, second college transferred to x3, pay-off to no-good boyfriend/girlfriend x3, wedding x3, nursing home for us at 50 x2 ..."

While the doctor was thinking:

"Triplets? There go the clinic's statistics!"

E. In Case You've Ever Wondered What the Opposite of "Random Acts of Kindness" Was

I've truly loved and respected the vast majority of medical personnel I've encountered (and who have endured me) throughout my bouts with infertility and pregnancy. But I've noticed that even some of the best, most dedicated among them occasionally make careless, dare I say, even insensitive remarks. I attribute this to the fact that they work all day every day embedded in highly emotional high-risk situations and perhaps once in a while forget that we, the patients, don't.

I bring up these "Reckless Acts of Stupidity" at this juncture because- hey look! Here come some now!

Minutes after finding out that I had entered the

IVF clinic as a single and was leaving as a foursome, I got dressed and walked into the hallway where the doctor stood with his little cardboard wheel of fortune calculating my due date. "August 30th" he said with a wink and a smile to which he added—("Reckless Act of Stupidity" Alert #1):

"You won't really make it that far. It will be a difficult pregnancy but it will be a short one."

Well that's a nice spin on the good news / bad news scenario.

"The bad news is: You'll have a miserably uncomfortable, possibly painful, possibly tragic high-risk pregnancy. The good news is: Your children will be born premature."

And what the hell was he smiling about? I laugh

at pretty much everything that I shouldn't. There was a news story about a bus on its way to a charity event overturning into a lake and killing an old man. The person they interviewed said:

"He died doing what he loved." Then my husband Lloyd said:

"What? Drowning?"

I laughed at that for a week. I'm laughing at it again now. But more than a decade later, I'm still not feeling the doctor's high-risk pregnancy humor.

Mere seconds after that upsetting encounter with him and his cardboard wheel, I walked past the nurses' station. A nurse I knew pretty well stood there writing notes.

"It's triplets." I told her.

(Reckless Act of Stupidity Alert #2) Without looking up and still jotting she said:

"It usually ends up as twins."

Are you kidding me? I just finished two years of trying to get pregnant including a year of fertility treatments with you people-- stomach injections, butt injections, blood tests, urine holding, wearing paper couture, cold nurses with warm hands, warm nurses with cold hands, early appointments with doctors yawning over my uterus... and this is how we're celebrating? With talk of pain, suffering, and certain death?

A week or two later, I went to the bathroom and out came a lot of blood. Of course we thought that was it. Nurse Cavalier and her thoughtless remark had been right: The triplets had become twins or one or worse. We rushed over for another ultrasound. Nope. They were all still present and accounted for and thumbing their embryonic noses at that nurse. I wondered if I could carry all three babies to term just to spite her. I felt like one of those really rich, really nasty, really old people who keeps living just to piss off their heirs.

F. I Was An Infertegnant. It's sort of like a turducken

Immediately following that initial positive pregnancy test, I became what the medical community calls infertegnant. (Again you're looking for a footnote?) I was a lame duck infertility patient stuck in that gynecological limbo between when the infertility clinic is done with you because you're finally pregnant but the OB/GYN doesn't want to know you yet because you're not quite pregnant enough. I think there is an unwritten contract that fertility doctors have with prenatal doctors:

"We'll keep her for the first six weeks. If she doesn't implode by then, she's all yours."

So I continued to go to the fertility clinic to make sure the pregnancy was still on. I've always wondered whether it was all just a ruse to use me for free advertising.

"You see that woman over there? That's Lori. She was infertile too until she came to Dr. Martin's fertility clinic. Now she's forty-one and pregnant! If she can do it, so can you!"

I'm guessing they wouldn't mention the whole "triplets" part.

Laughing *IS* Conceivable No Matter How Many You're Carrying

Chapter Two: Staying Pregnant with More than One Baby

My fertility doctor's final duty was to hand me off to a high-risk maternal-fetal doctor. (Wait. How did I just go from "not the least bit pregnant" to "high risk"? I had so much trouble getting pregnant. Now I was going to have trouble staying pregnant or having healthy kids or not dying in the process? This wasn't the pregnancy I signed up for. Where was the pregnancy where I gain ninety unnecessary pounds per baby just because I can and spend all day with my feet on Lloyd's lap while he rubs my Plantar warts?) The fertility doctor pointed with a pen to each of the three high-risk clinics on his list:

1) "This one is the best high-risk maternal-fetal

clinic in the business. They have state-of-the-art facilities, top-notch doctors, and are affiliated with all of the best hospitals in the area."

2) "And then there's this one that takes your insurance."

3) "And then there's this one that takes your insurance *and* is within a hundred miles of your home."

Don't get me wrong. The high-risk maternal-fetal place I ended up going to was amazing even if I did have to deal with:

A. "Dr. Doom"

Those post-knocked-up visits to the fertility clinic were by no means our first brush with negativity. I come from a long line of relatives whose unofficial cause of death was: "Drowning in a half-empty glass", and Lloyd's family have been devout pessimists for centuries. (Every time Lloyd tells his father how well his job is going his response is: "Oh, you're still there?")

But at that initial meeting, Dr. Doom brought negativity to a whole new level. You would have thought by listening to her that being pregnant with triplets could only end in disaster. There were no happy stories. It was a death sentence. I knew she was just doing her job and that everything she told us was probably legally and /or ethically required but that didn't stop me from picturing myself throttling her like Homer Simpson does to Bart as she spoke.

The most irritating part was how nonchalantly she talked about the risks. In fact, if memory serves, she was eating a chef salad out of a take-out tin as she spoke. Between chews and swallows, she hurled statistics at our heads like rocks. That's exactly what it felt like: A verbal stoning. (Call this: "Reckless Act of Stupidity" Alert #3)

"With triplets, there is a 30% chance one of your internal organs will explode during the pregnancy. 1 in 7 women has kidney failure... or her liver shuts down. (Tackling a green pepper between stats.) Or their kidneys shut down and their liver fails and then there are complications and they need spleen surgery. Or their appendix bursts. In fact, I've seen women who have had their appendix removed and it still bursts. And if you still have your tonsils, I wouldn't. I'm not going to go into what could happen but trust me, I just wouldn't have tonsils if I were you. And your blood pressure could go sky high and you or the babies could die. In fact, all of you could die. Or you could get gestational diabetes and one or more of you could die. Or you could have a stroke or a heart attack or male pattern baldness or jock itch or claustrophobia… and die. (Is that an onion?) Or you could have to go out alone in public with three infants and wish you were dead. Oh, you live up four flights of stairs? You'll have to move during the pregnancy. And you'll have to buy a van. (Should be winding up soon. Running out of ranch. Never enough in those dumb little cups.) And you'll have to stop working at five months. And you'll be hospitalized several times during the pregnancy. And when you're not in the hospital, you'll be on bed rest. And 8 out of 10 bedridden women who are pregnant with triplets turn onto their stomachs and accidentally smother themselves and die." As she folded up her empty tin and shoved it into the trash, I mumbled in my stupor:

"I've never heard of that happening."

"I'm not surprised. It happens so often it doesn't even make the news" she said matter-of-factly, tossing in the white take-out bag and pushing it down with her foot.

But Dr. Doom was not only great at spewing ranch and risks at us, she also had a solution to make all of the risks go away: Reduce the number of people inside of me. In fact, by the way, way back when, she, Dr. Doom, had done a reduction herself. (I'm assuming she meant that figuratively.)

It would solve all of our woes. The chance of one of us dying during a twin pregnancy was 1/3 of what it was during a triplet pregnancy. My blood pressure and blood sugar would only go twice as high as normal instead of three times as high. My lower spine would still splinter but chances were good I'd still have one working hip. I could learn to play the viola because studies have shown that women with twins are four times more likely to be good viola players than other women. I could work a month longer at my job and be hospitalized half as many times. I would be less of a social outcast (like going from having leprosy to a bad case of acne) as people would appreciate me forcing them to buy only two of everything for the baby shower instead of three, and we would be able to keep our two-door Chevy Cavalier and fourth floor elevatorless apartment instead of trading them both in for a houseboat... Oh and most important, not only can a family of four get on all of the rides together at Disneyland but at a restaurant, we wouldn't need that extra chair at the end of the table that every passerby bunks into going to and from the bathroom and kitchen.

Wow. If you don't count the seven pounds I've gained and lost thirty-two times, the only bodily reduction I'd ever thought about was taking my boobs down to a "C". Not only was I shocked, taken aback, and overall totally overwhelmed at the suggestion of reducing the number of people growing inside of me, I was also a tad miffed. With a sudden burst of self-confidence that came out of I don't know where, I told her:

"Look, the fertility clinic put three embryos in me and are pissed that I have three embryos in me. Then they shipped me off to you because you're a high-risk facility and now you're pissed because

I'm too high-risk. What do you people want from *me*? Take it up with each other!"

On one side of the desk Dr. Doom unmoved, moved on to her mocha latte. On the other side sat a barely pregnant-with-triplets woman, head on her knees, half nauseated from the pregnancy, half nauseated from the conversation, rocking back and forth and muttering to herself. (This was during a half-hour office visit. I'm guessing I wouldn't fare too well in a hostage situation.) Next to her, her loving husband handling the "It's a *Really* High-Risk Pregnancy, Charlie Brown!" news every bit as well as he did the "It's Triplets, Charlie Brown!" news, comforting her by saying nothing, staring into space, and trying his best to evaporate into the mocha latte vapor. (Less likely to get shot in a hostage situation. I imagine it's hard to aim at the invisible.) With no emotional, mental, or physical strength left, I left Dr. Doom with the strongest rejection of her embryo reduction idea I could muster at the moment: A firm "I doubt it." Our final decision was to be found inside a champagne bottle.

B. And I Was County Cork

Since I was forty-one plus when I got pregnant (or as the hateful medical community reveled in calling me: Forty-one years, three hundred and six days), it was recommended that I go for a CVS. Not knowing what that was, I naturally thought of the pharmacy. I hoped that I could just buy vitamins and a Snickers and leave with my freakishly long receipt with a coupon for two dollars off my next order of twenty-five dollars as long as my next order of twenty-five dollars was in the next two days. Turns out Chorionic Villus Sampling-- CVS to its friends-- is a test to detect genetic abnormalities in the fetus. It's similar to amniocentesis but it can be done earlier in the pregnancy with faster results. The samples were taken from the babies' placentas with what looked like a giant champagne bottle opener with my belly being the cork.

As I said, Lloyd and I were against reducing the number of embryos but decided to wait for these test results before making any final proclamations. If we'd had any really bad discoveries like somebody's arm was growing out of their eye, we may have been forced to re-think. And I would never criticize anyone who chooses reduction. I'm sure it has saved many lives. But I just couldn't shake the thought:

"What if they take out the only decent kid and leave us with two miserable ones?"

About a week and a half after the CVS test, I got a call from the nurse with the first baby's results. "Triplet B" was fine. And, yes, I did want to know the gender-- a girl. The Jewish tradition is to name your child after a deceased close relative. Sometimes we just use their first initial. This was a valuable loophole in naming Hayley since my mother, Harriet, hated her name. (Fun Fact: "Harriet" was really her middle name. When she was a kid she switched it with her first name "Edna" which she hated even more.)

A few days later, I got another call. The results were in for "Triplet C". Baby was fine--another girl. Then we waited. No results in yet for "Triplet A". At least another week went by. Finally on a

Friday afternoon about 4 p.m., I was resting in bed when I vaguely heard the answering machine pick up.

"Hi Lori. This is the nurse. I have the results back on "Triplet A". Give me a call on Monday."

Monday? I waited for this call for forever and this sadistic woman was going to leave me hanging over the weekend? Heeell no! You've never seen a woman carrying triplets either internally or externally move so fast through an obstacle course. Straddling the laundry basket, around the shoe pile, over the vacuum cleaner (yeah that one was a challenge). Luckily it was a Queens apartment so the phone in the living room and the bed in the bedroom were only eight feet apart. I got there in the nick of time.

"Hello? Hello? Don't hang up!"

"I think you'll be happy" she said. "It's a boy and he's fine."

I thought: "Sure he was fine before I hurdled over appliances. Now I might need some other test altogether."

So once the three CVS tests had all come back normal, our answer was officially, permanently, irrevocably stated: We were *not* going to do the embryo reduction. My boobs were still on the table and up for grabs but nobody seemed to care.

When I headed into my first legitimate appointment at the maternal-fetal clinic, (I refuse to count Dr. Doom's scared straight disorientation) I said to the lovely doctor:

"Well, I'm almost forty-two, I've never been pregnant and now I'm having triplets. I guess the only way I could be more high-risk is if you poured gasoline over me."

(I imagine Dr. Doom's response would have been:

"Oh, didn't I mention? Never go near a gas station during the pregnancy... or a lawnmower. The smell alone will give everyone brain damage.")

But this doctor said:

"Are you kidding? I get twenty-five year old women in here who are a hundred pounds overweight and have been drinking, smoking, and taking drugs for ten years and I'm supposed to undo all of it in seven months. You're high-risk because you're almost forty-two, never been pregnant and are having triplets? Piece of cake." I told you he was lovely. But there were still wars to wage at this clinic.

C. My Ultra Ultrasounds: When the Bill Comes, My Insurance Company Gets Up from the Table and Hides in the Bathroom

Don't get me wrong. I had good insurance. If I hadn't, I probably would have been stuck with a doctor who rents space from McDonald's and does exams at the drive-thru. So if you ever see a woman in the U.S. being handed a soda as she throws her legs out of her car window, you'll know she's thirsty, pregnant, and uninsured.

But I suspected very early on that my ultrasounds were something that my doctors' office and my insurance company would never see eye to eye (or uterus to uterus) on. The doctors planned to do several during the pregnancy due to my age, tripletness etc. The insurance company didn't see the need for more than one. I guess they thought Lloyd and I were trying to scam them into paying for extras so we could get a head start on our family photo album. You know what people always tell you: "They grow up so fast. Take lots of pictures!"

Even that one measly ultrasound didn't go off without a hitch. The insurance company gave me a list of approved places where I could have it done. I think one was "Manny's Flash and Splash Ultrasound & Carwash". Predictably, my doctors' office flatly rejected outsourcing my ultrasounds and entered whatever the medical code is for "screw off". Too bad. It might have been nice to have Lloyd waiting inside the shop following me from window to window as I went through the scan.

And thus began a spirited tennis match between the insurance company and the doctors' office in which I was initially the ball being smacked back and forth and ultimately the net left standing between them, twisting in the wind.

"Your doctors' office has to send the verification form."

"They sent it last month."

"We never received it. Have them fax it. I'll go stand by the fax machine to make sure I get it the second it comes over."

"Okay, she just sent it."

"She couldn't have just sent it. I'm standing by the machine and nothing came over. Which number did she send it to?"

"The 616 number you just gave me."

"I'm standing right here. She didn't send it."

"I'm standing right *here*. I saw her send it."

"I didn't get anything. Wait, let me see if there's paper in the machine. Has anyone gotten faxes off this machine today?! Okay, it's coming through now. Great! Wait, this is the old form."

"She says that was the old form."

"That's the only form I have. The office manager is out today. I don't know where she keeps the new forms. Could she send us a new new form?"

"Can you send her a new new form?"

"Stephanie handles that. Unfortunately she's on maternity leave until April… if she comes back."

Finally, after weeks of pleading my special ridiculously high-risk case and presenting proof of my special ridiculously high-risk case-- blood results, pregnancy test results, letters from my maternal-fetal doctor, letters from my manager at work, letters from my eighth grade guidance counselor, letters from my mother's nephew in Ohio--the insurance company assured me they would pay for all of my ultrasounds. My doctors' billing person, however, assured me that the insurance company would initially assure me that they would cover all of the ultrasounds but ultimately wouldn't cover anything but their own ass.

And oh how right the doctors' billing person proved to be. I, not the insurance company, ended up paying for all of my ultrasounds. I made the final payment with check number 720. The third grade field trip was 719.

The hallways of the maternal-fetal clinic always greeted me with sound effects: A loud symphony of ocean waves and beating hearts wafting from the monitors. It was soothing and eerie at the same time-- like reading Poe on the beach.

D. My Ultra Ultrasounds: Turn Left at the Ear. You Have Arrived at your Destination.

The ultrasound techs were fantastic. That didn't prevent them, however, from committing "Reckless Acts of Stupidity" (Alerts #4 and #5 in case you're keeping score). One told me:

"The babies aren't moving."

While I went into cardiac arrest and she gave me chest compressions to the beat of "Stayin' Alive", another tech gave me straw-to-mouth orange juice resuscitation and the babies began moving. Apparently they had been asleep.

Another day another technician. This one said:

"I can't hear his heartbeat."

As the stroke kicked in and my face went numb, I was just able to get in my request for her to kindly clarify. What she meant was that my son had his back turned and she couldn't get at his chest. No worries. Nothing a few trips to the neurologist and a little speech therapy couldn't fix.

My ultrasounds became somewhat useless as the pregnancy progressed. It got so crowded in there all anyone could detect was a cluster of naked people all over each other. (Similar to how someone once described Woodstock to me.) Towards the end, I stopped having ultrasounds altogether. Even the doctors gave up trying to sort out the three-baby pile-up but not before one uttered her own "Reckless Act of Stupidity" (Alert #6):

"Oh by the way, Baby 'C' pushed Baby 'B' out of the way. So now 'C' is 'B' and 'B' is 'C'." And I was like:

"What is this, a shell game? They've had names for months. You can't just switch them around!"

At least once a week, Lloyd and I took the thirty-five minute drive / schlep in Long Island traffic with me on my side the whole way for appointments. As my belly grew, I became less like a passenger and more like cargo. I would turn onto my hip as Lloyd pulled, shifted and maneuvered me into place securing me with the shoulder belt like he was transporting a mini fridge to his dorm.

E. The Return of Dr. Doom

With the frequency of my appointments and five doctors on staff, it was inevitable that one day my luck would run out and I'd draw the "Dr. Doom" tarot card again. Upon examination she said: "You're doing great." Knowing what she was capable of, I should have jumped off the table and bolted out of there yelling to Lloyd:

"Grab my clothes! I'll get dressed in the car!"

Instead I sat there like a dope and watched the cheery "you're doing great" doctor degenerate back into the harbinger of death. ("Reckless Act of Stupidity" Alert #7):

"...but..." she continued. "...we had a woman who was just like you, about the same number of weeks, also having triplets. Everything looked fine and then she went home, her cervix opened up and she lost the whole pregnancy."

While I stared at her, Lloyd stared at me, wondering how much time he had to morph from supportive husband into the security guy on *Jerry Springer*. More furious than curious, I asked her:

"And....? Is there something I should be doing to prevent that?"

"No. Not really."

Sooo you're telling me this cautionary tale... *why*? Call me selfish but if it's got nothing to do with me or my pregnancy--if there's nothing I can do to stop it from happening-- if your little "Once upon a time in a maternal-fetal clinic far far away" serves no purpose but to scare the crap out of me, you know what? Keep it to yourself. You want to be a storyteller? After work, go downtown and sign up for an open mike.

That was my last straw with Dr. Doom. Don't get me wrong. I'm sure she's an excellent obstetrician and I was so thankful to her for blocking the absurdly bright lights with her black cloak and cloud. But I'd had about enough of her graveside manner. On my way out of the office, I asked the receptionist-- although it probably came out more like a rhetorical threat:

"I'm not going to have *her* from now on, am I?" She said:

"No. The doctors work as a team. They all see every patient." I said:

"Well now she's seen me. So if you'd be so kind, let her never see me again." And twelve years and counting, so far so good.

I really didn't need the distraction of Dr. Doom at that moment. Believe me, I had plenty of other issues to keep me entertained.

F. Your Typical, Run-of-the-Mill Pregnancy Annoyances: You Name It, It Annoyed Me

Hemorrhaging

Okay, bleeding. For the first few months, I was bleeding every day. When it first happened, panic-stricken (because who wouldn't be?) I called the doctor who told me casually:

"Of course you're bleeding. Your hormone levels

are really high."

Uh, okay. Could someone have mentioned that possibility before I, you know, freaked out?

Heartburn

I figured I could handle it one of two ways:

1) Like my sister-in-law did during all of her pregnancies: Announce every ten minutes: "It's the worst pain of my life. I feel like I'm going to die." Or:

2) Pop a Pepcid and call it a day. Since I'd rather not repeat myself six times an hour, I opted for #2.

Morning Sickness

You know how it subsides after the first trimester? I sure don't. As the babies grew and monopolized the region, I envisioned all of my vital organs cowering in a corner praying for it all to be over. By month five, digestion was no longer an option. It was like I'd had a gastric baby bypass. (Although I preferred to think of myself as a grand Victorian lady wearing a fashionable triplet corset.) For most of the pregnancy, I had the unenviable sensation of starving and being nauseated at the same time. Maybe that's why I love fast food so much. Every time I eat it, it brings up… those warm memories.

Shortness of Breath

No big deal. I just hung out at the dog park and hoped nobody would notice that the panting sound was coming from me.

Prenatal Congestion

From almost day one of the pregnancy, I sniffled. I let people assume whatever they wanted.

"Poor pregnant girl can't take her allergy medicine."

"Poor pregnant girl is weepy."

I know it made me see my coworkers who had been pregnant in a whole new light.

"Hmm. So maybe they're not all coke addicts."

I went online to see how long this annoyance would last and there it was:

"Pre-natal Congestion- Usually ends at childbirth."

Great. Eight months of sucking in air through my mouth between pants. Every day I was practicing Lamaze without even meaning to. No joke. The second all three babies were out of me, the first new mom, miracle of birth, waited forty-two years for this, better-write-them-down-in-a-journal-as-a-memento-for-the-kids words out of my mouth were:

"Hallelujah, I can breathe."

34 Weeks and Counting of Sexless Days and Nights

The only ones who ever ventured below my bra line were doctors and ultrasound techs. I looked upon them with the same pity I usually reserve for dental hygienists and pedicurists. Oh the horrors they must witness in the course of a career! Even my better half wanted no part of my bottom half. The doctors said it was fine to have sex during my first trimester but since I was bleeding the whole time, there were no takers. Later on we were told that we could have sex as long as I didn't enjoy it.

"Enjoying it" might cause uterine contractions. So while I spent the ride home that day picturing myself ordering ice cream and throwing it away, having the best body of my life in a world with no mirrors, and buying a racecar that never leaves the garage, my compassionate husband broke the silence.

"But your hands and mouth are still good to go, right?"

Oh my Aching Back, Hips, Shoulders, Knees and Toes, Knees and Toes

I won't say my spine was curved during the pregnancy but I looked like I was in constant search of a limbo pole to duck under. Lloyd took a lot of photos around this time. I suspect it was less out of affection for the mother of his impending children and more of a Loch Ness monster thing.

"Nobody will believe it unless I have proof!"

(I exaggerate not. He confessed to once waking up in the middle of the night, seeing me, a shadowy mass skulking around the apartment and mumbling: "Whoa. What the hell is that?")

For those times when I did venture out, Lloyd jostled me around the broken sidewalks of Astoria in a rented wheelchair. It just made sense. I could still walk okay but my feet moved twice as fast as my body like an obese Pomeranian. Not to mention, for a variety of safety reasons it is highly inadvisable to walk around NYC in full limbo pose looking up at the sky.

Besides the romantic rented wheelchair gift, Lloyd got me a fab body pillow that could be used in any sleep position. (Although obviously lying on my stomach was out unless I wanted to sleep three feet above the bed.) I usually wound the pillow around my legs. Taking the strain off my hips, it bought me an hour or two of sleep then I would have to rearrange it to find a new bearable position. Sometimes it looked like I was wrestling an intruder. Sometimes like I was paddling a surfboard. Speaking of water:

A hot shower running down my backbone. Mmmm. I would have loved a nice bath but getting me in and out of the tub would have required scaffolding and day laborers. I also would have loved the pool but summer coincided with my third trimester and I have enough trouble finding a bathing suit that fits when I'm not eight months pregnant with triplets. Speaking of apparel:

Am I Allowed to Include on This List of Pregnancy Annoyances, "Shopping for Maternity Clothes"?

I know. Why get pricy maternity garb when you can just stretch out the clothes of the guy who got you this way? Well, I figured I'd only be pregnant once and maybe I should get a couple of items to keep as souvenirs. The problem was that I was like microwave popcorn: Every time you looked at me, I had grown a little bigger. I stood in the store like a fool thinking:

"What size do I get? The size I am now or the size I'll be ten minutes from now?"

I ended up with shirts with non-committal dimensions ("M" and "L"), a few dresses that fit me on top with a belly area that flared out to infinity, and a nursing bra that I still haven't figured out. I never bought maternity panties but maybe I should have. Circa seven months, my husband side-glanced me sporting my usual Hanes ladies briefs which I admit, were looking a lot briefer than usual. He inquired lovingly yet rhetorically:

"You're asking an awful lot out of that underwear aren't you?"

Dressing for Dinner

My sister's friend gave me a pair of pregnancy shorts with that stretchy band across the stomach. No. Absolutely not. I mean I wear them all the time *now*. To me, they're not really "maternity shorts" as much as "buffet shorts". But during the pregnancy, I dressed myself exclusively from the waist up. Below that, whatever happened happened. Most of the time I had a big enough belly obstruction that I couldn't see anything beneath my boobs. I took that as a sign that whatever was going on down there was really none of my business.

The Mother of All Annoyances: No Guarantees--Money-Back or Otherwise

Just like--despite us enduring a year of being mentally, physically, emotionally and financially drained and all of their best efforts--nobody at the fertility clinic could guarantee that I would ever get pregnant, nobody at the high-risk maternal-fetal clinic could guarantee that I would stay pregnant, have healthy babies, or much of anything else no matter how much I begged for reassurance. Finally the doctors gave me a mantra:

"Just make it to twenty-eight weeks. Just make it to twenty-eight weeks."

I mean it wasn't exactly Deepak Chopra but at least it was something positive to shoot for. Upon reaching that milestone, I toddled into the doctors' office excitedly. Was there a non-alcoholic champagne celebration waiting for me? No. Just another doctor to tell me:

"Fine. Now just make it to thirty-two weeks."

And as you can probably tell, I always do as I'm told so I made it to thirty-two weeks...and then some.

G. Dr. Doom's Words Still Loomed. But How Many of Her Predictions Actually Came True?

Yes, I had a zillion pregnancy annoyances but what about all of the dire emergencies that Doom had seen in her crystal stethoscope?

Prediction #1: You'll Have to Buy a Bigger Vehicle- Perhaps the Partridge Family Bus is Available (Yes)

Not that we needed her to tell us that it would be better to buy a minivan in lieu of jamming the five of us and three rear-facing infant seats into our two-door Chevy clown car. It just seemed like better parenting to actually climb into the back of a vehicle to get the infants out instead of yanking them over the front seat.

Prediction #2: You'll Have to Move (not your bowels-the iron pills quashed any hope of that) (No)

If you recall, the good doctor said we would have to uproot ourselves from our apartment because walking up and down those forty-eight steps would cause me to implode. The arrangements were all set. My wonderful friend Roberta said we could temporarily either stay with her or switch apartments. As Lloyd and I mulled over these options, it occurred to me that nobody had mentioned the "moving thing" lately and thought maybe I should bring it up. A non-Doom doctor said:

"Why are you moving? You're fine."

I'm glad I asked before I headed over to Roberta's carrying my dresser.

So for the rest of the pregnancy, I just kept doing what I had been doing whenever I went out. I walked up half a flight of stairs at a time then sat on the steps and read letters and bills. At first my neighbors were amused by the mail-opening triplet-carrying sideshow. But by month seven, I had blossomed into Jabba the Pregnant Hutt from 4D-- a human road block impeding their way to both their apartments above and even more worrisome, the exit below. Nobody voiced their concerns but I could hear a few of them in their apartments opening their windows and testing out the fire escape ladder.

Prediction #3: You'll Have to Quit Your Job (I will if you will, Dr. Doom) (Yes)

Having not changed much from the waist up during the pregnancy, I really enjoyed chatting with coworkers who hadn't seen me in a while then rolling my chair back from the desk and watching their faces contort. Nevertheless, I did quit working at five months like Doom presumed because I was dead tired and felt the Universe summoning me to my couch and stack of *US* magazines. Being alone in the apartment all day, I discovered two things about myself: 1) I have a great talent for picking stuff up with my toes 2) I could no longer walk between any two pieces of furniture without inadvertently taking at least one of them with me.

One evening, when my husband came home from work, it looked like I'd spent the day with a poltergeist: The kitchen chair was in the hallway, the night table in the bathroom. He said:

"You really shouldn't be rearranging furniture." Like that was the decor I'd be going for.

"Are you for real?" I said. "I got up to make soup and this is what I got."

I did return to work at eight months--for my baby shower anyway. I overheard my boss, Maureen, saying the nicest thing I ever heard a boss say about me behind my back:

"Wow. I thought she would be a lot bigger."

Prediction #4: You'll Have Several Hospital Stays (No)

One night at about six months, I woke up at 4 a.m. to go to the bathroom and noticed a few specks of blood. As per the doctor on call, we went to the emergency room to get it checked out. Apparently my son's placenta had nicked my uterine wall. Goodnight and goodbye. My "hospital stay" lasted forty-five minutes.

Predictions #5/6, 7, 8, & 9: You'll Have High Blood Pressure/Preeclampsia, Gestational Diabetes, Pre-Term Labor and Be On Bed Rest (No/No, No, No, and No.)

120 / 80. No diabetes. Not a single contraction.

None.

At thirty-two weeks, I went to the hospital for steroid shots to help the babies' lungs develop just in case I didn't make it to thirty-three weeks when they develop on their own. The kids were running out of growing room so they decided to keep me. They figured that scheduling a c-section, assembling all of the necessary medical personnel and prepping the operating room would take less time than Lloyd tethering me back into the car.

Laughing *IS* Conceivable No Matter How Many You're Carrying

Chapter Three: Giving Birth to More Than One Baby

A. Re-Enacting the Stateroom Scene from *A Night at the Opera:* My Hospital (1/3 of a) Room

For the better part of my two week hospital stay, I shared a 9 x 12 room--a mere manila envelope of a room--with two other girls. It was like my college dorm all over again. Isn't it amazing how a situation can be so cool when you're eighteen and lose its coolness completely when you're forty-two and pregnant with triplets?

A nearby hospital had recently closed so we got the overflow. Both of the other women had already given birth--one with twin boys who were in the dorm room with us. The other woman stayed to have surgery. And then there was me, the mini-fridge parallel-parked by the window.

The only things separating us were those curtains that wind around a track. They keep the viewing private for the puppet show going on inside but are neither smell-proof nor sound-proof. During one visit, the surgery girl's curvaceous aunt whispered to her:

"That woman's belly hasn't gone down at all."

To which her niece replied:

"That's because it's triplets and she hasn't had them yet."

Meanwhile over in my 1/3 of the room, the doctor, Lloyd, and I were chatting when suddenly Auntie's entire curtain-covered back half jutted into my area narrowly missing Lloyd. Apparently she was unaware that just because you are inside the curtain doesn't mean you're still in your 1/3 of the room. Lloyd, being the consummate gentleman, gently nudged her--curtain, chair and all--back over to her side. (I was hoping he wouldn't slip under her like I once did pushing my car off the ice.) She kept on gabbing, paying no attention to the man behind the curtain or the chair-on-tile screeching noise that sounded like a freight train hitting the brakes.

I said to the doctor:

"Welcome to my suite at the Ritz." He rolled his eyes.

"More like a Ritz cracker."

There actually were some similarities to a luxury hotel: Air conditioning, cable TV and meals all for a mere $1000 a day. Box of Tissues: $26. Two Tums: $109. Dr. T. Fisher: $1500. Who is Dr. T. Fisher? As far as I know, the only place he or she ever showed up was on my itemized bill. Of course there was room service. Nobody would dare let me go into public areas in my two hospital gowns-one on the front that tied in the back and one on the back that tied in the front-in a feeble attempt to cover my entire panorama. I finished off the ensemble with neon yellow skid-proof socks.

Lloyd stayed with me in the hospital every night. I'm sure this was out of sheer devotion and not because, mid heat wave, the electric company had cut power making our top floor Queens apartment a balmy 210 degrees Fahrenheit.

Neither of us pretended that sharing the hospital bed was a possibility. How cozy that would have been: Just Lloyd, me, our three internal children, my doll Rutie, my body pillow, and mounds of sheets and blankets to prop up various body parts. I looked like the victim of a door buster sale at Bed Bath & Beyond.

Lloyd agreed to let me have the bed. He slept on the floor next to me on a futon chair turned bacon-strip-of-a-cot. If chivalry hadn't stepped in, gravity would have. Once I got down there, there would have been no getting me up. If a hurricane had hit,

I'm sure the staff, scrambling to get everyone to safety, would have glanced over at me and said "She'll be fine" and closed the door. Besides, anyone bending over to examine me would have looked like they were administering last rites, which is never good for patient morale.

So this was the scene every night: Down there on his futon strip we had my husband who, due to back issues, doesn't get up too fast but sort of sits up in stages like an adjustable chaise lounge at the beach. He is also a sound sleeper and has less than perfect hearing. And way up there, two stories above him perched atop a hospital bed, was an overly pregnant woman prone to frequent urinations.

And considering the size of me and the size of my third of the room, there was only one route to the restroom: Over Lloyd. And considering the view from his vantage point as I straddled over him in my bottomless Michael Kors couture double hospital gown wrap dress, it was kind of nice that it was my husband down there and not the cleaning woman reaching under my bed with her Swiffer. (And I had to keep reminding myself he *was* down there so I wouldn't trip over him or use his head as a step ladder.)

That first night, Lloyd realized that "for better or worse" included being awoken at 2 a.m. by a hospital gown tie grazing his hairline and seeing unspeakable things in the darkness. A thoughtful wife would have tapped him with her yellow neon toe and asked him to stand or at the very least whisper-shouted:

"Whatever you do, don't look up!"

As I finished in the bathroom and exited, Lloyd flipped himself over facedown. I've never seen anyone in a room not engulfed in flames hold a pillow to their face with such force. Perhaps he had chosen to smother himself rather than relive the trauma on my return trip. I looked around for alternate routes. Hmm. I could walk through the hallway into the next room, climb out their window, leap from their sixth floor ledge to my sixth floor ledge and lower myself down through my window. Or I could just go back the way I'd come, over Lloyd, and hope I made it before he suffocated. I hustled along as fast as anyone could with fourteen pounds of people in them so I wouldn't have to give any awkward explanations to those people when they got older.

"No. I never said your father died during

childbirth. It was in the hospital room the night before."

In case you think I've been exaggerating about how cramped my manila envelope room was... Besides us three roomies, there were two husbands, two babies externally and three babies internally. And then there was the twenty-four hour parade of transients. Mercifully, most of our family only poked their heads in so they could tell everyone they visited then said "We'll let you rest" and evaporated. Vendors floated in and out all day and night selling baby bracelets, baby photos... It was a dream gig for a door-to-door salesman. Through the ajar door, behind the curtain, awaited a mostly naked woman under the sheets. If I hadn't had my husband on the floor and been eight and a half months pregnant with triplets, it could have been the start of a beautiful porno movie. As it was, I was the perfect captive audience for every sales pitch and hospital employee who happened by. I was tempted to turn off the lights and leave a bowl of fun-size candy outside the door.

Reckless Act of Stupidity #8 Comes to Call

Being a New Yorker, I always wake up when someone enters my space. One night, all I could see through the blackness were the glaring red numbers of a blood pressure machine: "185 over 100". I popped up like a Fisher Price farm animal and yelled out:

"What's happening?! Why is it so high?!"

The nurse whispered calmly as she tugged the Velcro on the arm cuff:

"That's from the last person. I haven't even started you yet."

Between breaths in and out of a paper bag I asked:

"And now you're going to take my blood pressure? How would you guess *that's* going to go?"

And all the while my hard of hearing Prince Charming slept. Poor Lloyd. People kept trying to swipe his futon strip because there weren't enough to go around. So while most people make their bed when they get up, Lloyd walked around the hospital all day with his flung over his shoulder.

A day or two into my hospital stay, it finally dawned on me that nobody had ever mentioned how the babies were going to get out of my uterus and into the minivan. I thought maybe I should bring it up. Even though everything looked fine, the doctors said they always advised against delivering twins, triplets, etc. naturally for fear that one would get trapped behind a contraction. I had the best "labor" in history. The anesthesiologist asked:

"Mrs. Fox, are your legs getting warm?"

A while later someone brought me three newborns. All in all, my birthing experience resembled pizza delivery more than baby delivery.

B. Re-enacting the Stateroom Scene from *A Night at the Opera* Part II: The Deliverance

There's the old wives' tale that babies arrive in the middle of the night. Not if it's a scheduled c-section to remove thirty-four week triplets. I was wheeled in bright and early at 8 a.m. so the staff would be fresh for the arduous task ahead. How many people are in the average hospital delivery room? A doctor, a nurse, a spouse, maybe another family member? Four or five total? Mine had twenty-two people. Around me were the doctor, the resident assisting her, Lloyd, and the anesthesiologist. Waiting in the wings were three medical teams: One team for each baby. There were pediatricians, pediatric surgeons, pediatric nurses, a waterless cookware salesman who had tracked me down, some street performers... (I tossed coins into their guitar case between babies "A" and "B".)

At first I wasn't too sure about the anesthesiologist since he had trouble finding my spine or at least the part of it he required. By the third poke, I checked to make sure the picture on his hospital ID matched. By the fourth poke, I checked to make sure his surgical cap hadn't slipped down over his eyes. Not that any of this was his fault. Apparently, just like my delivery room, my hospital room, and my uterus before them, my vertebrae were unreasonably crowded with zero space to slip in a needle. In an attempt to get the bones to separate, he set a pillow on my giant belly and pushed my head down on it like the top graham cracker in a S'mores. Then, syringe pointed at my backbone, he looked to me for guidance which tells you just how empty his bag of tricks really was.

"Am I in the right spot?" he inquired.

"No, you're a little off to the left."

"Are you sure? I think this is the spot."

"Trust me. You're off to the left." Typical man.

That Red Stuff on the Floor Ain't No Ocean Spray

The moment the doctor and her resident arrived I knew it wasn't going to be pretty. I had a hunch that the hip boots they were wearing were not for a post-surgery field trip to a cranberry bog. But I have to say, my triplet delivery struck the perfect balance. I didn't sleep through my children's birth as my mother had decades before and yet I was on the tidy side of the curtain blissfully unaware of the bloody battle being waged down south. Lloyd wasn't so lucky. I could see him mentally debating whether to run out of the room and miss the once-in-a-lifetime triple miracle of his children's birth or throw up in his mask. He found a happy medium. He kind of fainted without falling. After that, I'm not sure he remembered he was there let alone that I was. (Well, you saw how he handled "It's

Triplets!" and "It's a High-Risk Pregnancy!" Did anyone really expect him to go Zen at: "It's a C-Section *Right There*, Charlie Brown!"?)

I couldn't see anything but I could hear everything. At one point, the doctor said to the resident trying to sound unflustered:

"Cut there. No. Not there." I thought:

"And there goes my brake line."

McDonald's cashier, dentist's receptionist, obstetrician... Why oh why do I always get the trainee?

Help from the Blindfolded Guy

He may not have impressed me with his "Pin the tail on Lori's spine" routine, but once the show got going, the anesthesiologist was my greatest ally.

The doctor and resident never stopped to chat and Lloyd had long since faded into Madame Tussauds mode looking very life-like but unable to move or speak. But the anesthesiologist was a pro. He gave me the play-by-play without the color commentary. The nice G-rated version- no violence, strong language, or sexual situations.

"They just took out the first baby. Now the nurse is taking him over to his team. You'll be able to see him in a minute."

He was so informative and yet so soothing. Like Mr. Rogers with a syringe and a mask. I half-expected the baby to be brought to me via trolley. As each child emerged, I heard what sounded more like quacking than crying. And the quacking kept getting louder and louder.

My son Jacob came out first at 8:51. For sixty whole seconds he was an only child. He regularly refers to this as "the best minute of my life." Carly was born at 8:52 followed by Hayley at 8:54. And Jacob's euphoria was forever extinguished.

As they rolled me out of the delivery room past Lloyd, I told him he was going to awaken feeling refreshed then counted to three and snapped my fingers. Had I known the gruesome acts to come in the recovery room, I might have left him in his trance a while longer. A lovely young nurse gently pressed on my abdomen. Then the veteran walked over.

"You can't do it like that. You have to get the clots out of her."

She grabbed a fistful of my baby flap and wrung it

out like a T-shirt I'd just swum in. What a way to find out your epidural had worn off. But the old nurse was happy. She said to the other one:

"There! See?"

Luckily, I couldn't. Sometimes I have to close one eye when I see what comes out of a *Chopped* basket. And I fear whatever came out of me was far worse.

C. Tiptoeing Through Medical Minefields

Shortly after I was returned to my hospital room, one of the doctors came in:

"You lost a lot of blood. You might need a transfusion."

Then someone handed me my liquid lunch menu, I sent Lloyd on a mission to score an ample supply of hospital Jell-O and everybody went on with their day. A while later, another doctor told me:

"Your son's placenta was stuck to your uterus. That could cause an infection. We might have to go back in."

Then someone handed me my liquid dinner menu, I sent Lloyd on a mission to replace the disappointing orange Jell-O he had come back with earlier and everybody went on with their evening. And I was left to ponder:

"So…Am I bleeding to death? Do I need another operation? Neither? Both?"

Just like the major "you'll have to move to a new apartment" warning, the transfusion and infection bombshells were casually detonated in front of me and never brought up again. The next morning, I finally hailed down a doctor.

"So are you doing this transfusion thing or what?"

"No, you're fine."

"What about the placenta infection surgery thing?"

"No, that's fine too."

"Great. Did it ever occur to anybody to let me know?"

It may sound like I was totally ungrateful for the good news but having been left overnight to stew in a pot full of post-partum hormones and "what ifs", it was a lot nicer than what I really wanted to do--smile and yell after him in a big, cheery voice:

"Fuck you for not telling me! Have a nice day!"

Hours after giving birth, Lloyd wheeled me into the Neonatal Intensive Care Unit (NICU). As we put on masks and scrubbed our hands in the outer room, I noticed a woman by the first bassinette holding a baby with a little pink hat. I said:

"Aw, did you just have her?" She said:

"No, Mrs. Fox. You did."

You've heard of postpartum depression. Is there such a thing as postpartum denial?

D. My Husband Teaches Me My ABCs

The babies had been put straight into the NICU because of their sizes: Jacob: 4 lbs. 15 ozs., Carly: 4 lbs. 10 ozs., Hayley: 3 lbs. 9 1/2 ozs. Lloyd educated me:

"The rooms go 'A' through 'D'. Two of them are in 'D' and one is in 'C'."

I hyperventilated.

"That's terrible! Why aren't they in 'A' & 'B'?!" Yet another maternal freak out because nobody explained anything. Lloyd said:

"No no I think 'D' is where they go when they're almost ready to go home."

"Oh. That's good. But this is terrible! What's wrong with my other child?!"

"Nothing's wrong with her."

"I don't believe you! If nothing is wrong with her why is she in 'C'?!"

"Because someone had triplets and they ran out of room in 'D'."

All in all they were doing great. Jacob had a little jaundice and a feeding tube because he wasn't eating fast enough. Maybe they should have let him wander around the room with his food as he's done every meal since.

The doctors said I could be released from the hospital as soon as I "passed air from below". Now why can't life be like that? If you're trapped in a three hour meeting at work, a teacher's conference, a conversation with your yenta neighbor--all you have to do is fart and they'll let you leave. Nobody in my house would ever have to stay anywhere for more than ten minutes.

E. My First Eviction Notice

Every parent with a child in the NICU can't wait to bring them home...except me. I was exhausted and extremely weak. My children may have weighed in at under five pounds apiece but every time I picked one up I pulled muscles in both arms. Regardless, four days after I had three people removed from my body, as I lay in the bed like a deflated beach ball barely strong enough to point the remote at the TV, the doctor announced that "Baby B" and I were ready to go home. I begged to differ.

"Well," I told him, "she can go wherever she wants but I'm not budging" as I, a life-long Mets fan, turned up the volume on the Yankee game. The doctor, defeated, left the room mumbling something about anemia buying me another day with the insurance company. And as awful as it sounds, since the kids were doing fine, I actually preferred they stay a little longer too. I figured the professional round-the-clock care was worlds better than what they would currently get at home: A shell-shocked wax figure father and a mother with the physical strength of a newspaper left on the driveway in the rain. (Those plastic bags never work.)

F. Eviction Day

So Carly, the baby formerly known as "Baby B", formerly formerly known as "Baby C" who was scheduled to go home with me on Day 4, left with me on Day 5. "Baby A" aka Jacob was also ready to be sprung on Day 5 but nobody told us (surprised?) so we didn't have his car seat set up and had to drive all the way back with Carly the next day to get him.

Meanwhile, my mother-in-law had come up from Florida for the birth, didn't feel well, was diagnosed with end stage cancer and put into hospice care all within the week. Lloyd drove two hours each way every day to the far reaches of Long Island to visit her, dropping off whatever breast milk I could eke out for Hayley at the hospital along the way.

Hayley was discharged a few days later. I couldn't

muster the energy to walk through that hospital yet again let alone up the forty-eight steps in our building. I stayed home with the two babies while my friend Roberta went in my place. Lloyd left her in the double-parked minivan as he raced in to retrieve Hayley before hospital security came by since Roberta was in the back row of the van awaiting the baby and didn't know how to drive.

As I welcomed home my final newborn, I thought to myself:

"I'm going to take care of all of these babies? Are you kidding? I need someone to take care of *me*."

Not to say that we were already burned out mere days after bringing the babies home, but in the wee hours, immediately following diaper changes, Lloyd and I sat in the living room debating which one of us was holding the only boy. Nothing is as obvious as it should be at 3 a.m.

Laughing *IS* Conceivable No Matter How Many You're Carrying

Chapter Four: Taking Care of More Than One Baby aka Getting From the NICU to Nick Jr.

Before they were born, Lloyd and I didn't fully appreciate that we were about to trade in our jobs for work on a twenty-four hour energy sucking, body ravaging, soul torturing, baby assembly line. Feeding, diaper. Feeding, diaper. Feeding, diaper. Luckily we had loads of laundry, mixing formula, and scrubbing breast pumps to break up the monotony. Then there was the constant crying and shrieking and Baby Houdini to deal with. When we finally had everyone swaddled and tried to tip-toe out of the room to safety, out of the corner of my eye, I'd see that arm pop up out of the bassinette. Lloyd has poor peripheral vision and overall I think it's made him a happier parent.

A. Re-Enacting the Stateroom Scene from *A Night at the Opera* Part III: The Pediatrician's Office

When they were a week and a half old, we took the babies to their first doctor's appointment where we were escorted into a tiny examination room. I thought:

"This has been my kids' whole life so far. They went from a cramped uterus to a cramped hospital room to a cramped delivery room to a cramped apartment to a cramped examination room. They must think we live in a very crowded country."

In this ear-splittingly noisy minuscule room, there

was one doctor, two nurses, three screaming children and two parents who had aged ten years in nine days who undressed and re-dressed baby after baby while the nurses asked over and over:

"Is this one Hayley?" to which I finally replied in my wiped-out worn-out whisper:"Who cares?" Then I turned to the doctor:

"How long before they sleep through the night?" Hoping against hope that he'd say: "Tomorrow-- Tuesday of the latest." Instead he said:

"Around five months."

With eyes closed and leaning against Lloyd, my rock who was weaving like the balloon guy in front of the car dealership, I responded.

"That's okay. We'll be dead way before then."

We certainly had nobody but ourselves (and maybe modern medicine) to "blame" for us going from a couple to a family of five in three minutes or from two full-time incomes to barely any. Having said that, I feel the need to issue the following disclaimer:

"The section you are about to read makes me sound like an ungrateful, resentful woman who was trying to shirk her responsibilities as a new mother whenever possible. To be clear…" Oh great. Now I forgot what I was going to say.

B. Help is on the Way… Not to *Us*… Maybe to a Tornado or Something

When Lloyd had walked up that forty-eighth step to our apartment to bring home that final baby, I flung the front door open to welcome them and to usher in the long line of nobody behind them who came to help us. This included five sisters and a cousin the farthest of whom lived an hour and a half away.

One of them stopped by for "just a quick visit".

So nice to see her.

"May I get you a beverage while I'm hunched over the tub bathing three babies, soaking my sore breasts, and doing last Wednesday's dishes?"

Another's total contribution was her saying "I know it's hard" nine times in a ten minute phone conversation.

A third, after several proddings, finally agreed to take me to my six week check-up. As we left my apartment headed for the forty-eight steps, I slung my oversized, overstuffed diaper bag over my shoulder and grabbed an infant-filled carrier in each hand. I stared at the relative then at the remaining infant-filled carrier on the floor. Then back at the relative. Then back at the carrier. Finally I said:

"You need both hands to carry your keys?"

"I really don't feel comfortable carrying a baby" she explained. "Maybe I could just take your pocketbook."

We Accept Cash, Checks, and All Major and Minor Baby Items (aka: "Making Use of the Useless")

Reliable help with newborns is priceless but if you're not reliable or willing to help who says you can't put a price on friendship? Sure you can. Can of formula $22.50. There you go. See how easy that was? One family member fought back:

"I already gave you diapers at the baby shower." I set her straight.

"Yeah, okay. That was over a month ago. A bowel movement isn't a bar mitzvah. You don't have only one in your lifetime."

Don't get me wrong. I wasn't requesting really big ticket items. I wasn't even telling anyone to spend money to make their useless selves useful.

"Hey, those are some nice onesies you've got stacked on your dryer. Well, you had your tubes tied. And your son's in ninth grade... Just sayin'."

And to those of you who adamantly refused to be persuaded out of your uselessness, twelve years later we're still friends. We're still family. For you my door remains forever open--as does my gift registry.

Yet Another Reason I Love New England

While no family members ran to our aid, my friend Ida pitched in for a full twenty-four hours. (I'm thinking it wasn't a pleasant experience for her though. She hasn't spoken to me since.) And my friend Sharon helped immensely all the way from Massachusetts. She hired a doula in my area. (A woman who assists midwives and new mothers. Don't worry. I didn't know either.) She got the babies on sleeping and feeding schedules and watched them while we slept in hopes of extending our lives another week. When Sharon's money ran out, I just couldn't let my doula go. I paid her until she had to leave for another assignment then literally emptied my bank account to finance a string of half-assed, overpriced, astonishingly-worth-it-when-you're-desperate baby nurses. One showed up an hour late every day. One argued that there were two teaspoons in a tablespoon. Since the pediatrician and I agreed that none of my four pound children needed to slim down, I cracked open my old *Joy of Cooking* to prove that "3 teaspoons = 1 tablespoon" is actually a fact and not just my opinion as she had suggested.

There are No Atheists in Foxholes or Baby Fox Assembly Lines

Besides Sharon's fabulous doula present, we got some other wonderfully unexpected assistance. A small faith-based non-profit in Flushing Queens prayed for us in their office and gave us whatever items they had. And one evening after our doula had moved on, three young women from her church--total strangers to us--just showed up. They handed us a gift card bought with money they had collected then watched the babies all night so we could rest.

I must say though, during this period in our lives, organized religion was very hit or miss. In a glorious speech to the congregation, our synagogue's president announced that in honor of the new Fox triplets, as a gift from their family to ours, a tree would be planted in Israel!

Lovely sentiment. And………?

So what kind of tree are you planting? Is it something I can puree? Or what say we compromise? You forget about the tree altogether and we'll let you plant a box of diapers on our doorstep instead. Deal?!

After the service, this lovely lady named Lotte who had twins in their fifties came over to us and slipped me a twenty-five dollar Target gift card. I could have kissed her on her bright pink lips.

Back when I did my baby registry, I went to scan an item three times. The guy working there grabbed my wrist:

"Whoa. You already did that one!"

Lloyd said something he hasn't said once in the twelve years since I gave birth:

"Leave her alone. She knows what she's doing.

C. "3 Against 2" Starts to Look Pretty Good

It wasn't long before Lloyd and Lori versus The Triplets turned into just them and me. Having taken time off to stay with me in the hospital and visit his mother in hospice (and attend her funeral when the babies were two weeks old), Lloyd had no choice but to return to work. One day I called him crying hysterically.

"I can't take this anymore! I can't be alone with them in the apartment all day with the constant noise! I just can't! I have to leave!"

He told me to call my neighbor across the hall. She said she would be right over. I'm still waiting. Lloyd came home early and didn't leave for work again until the kids started school. To show my gratitude for all of his hard work and dedication, when the babies were two months old, I wished him all the best and went back to my job. Women struggle all the time with leaving their infants to return to work. Are you kidding me? It was the break I had been waiting for.

We didn't venture far from home with the newbies at first. In fact, we only brought them downstairs to the front of our building to escape our stifling, ear drum piercingly loud, diaper stench of an apartment. Lloyd and I parked the babies in their carriers on the sidewalk lined up against the building and sat on the stoop next to them. It looked like we were having a yard sale. We called out to passersby: "Three for a dollar!" and "Buy two get one free!"

D. Sight-Seeing in NYC is Lots of Fun...And What a Sight We Were

When the triplets were born, my cousin the pediatrician told us it was okay for them to be outside "as long as you don't let people get too close to them." We may as well have stayed home until the first day of pre-school. Do you have any idea what it's like trying to keep people from crowding around infant triplets? When we pushed them around the neighborhood in their six foot long stretch limousine stroller, people flocked from the other side of Steinway Street. And it takes a lot to get New Yorkers to flock. Some wanted photos. Lloyd referred to them as "The Poor Man's Paparazzi". Some made comments:

"Well, you survived."

"Who says so?"

Others asked questions:

"Is it hard?"

"Look at us. We're only twenty-two."

"Why don't you dress the girls alike?"

"Because they're two different people."

"Are they all boys?"

"Yes. The one with the blue blanket is a boy. And so is the one with the pink blanket... and the other one with the pink blanket." (Did you even look?)

"Did you have them vaginally?"

Oh my Gd. This total stranger just said my body part out loud. Shouldn't our privates be like the Girl Scouts in front of Wal-Mart? Just because we all know they're there doesn't mean we have to publicly acknowledge them.

"Are the girls identical?"

"Lady, at three in the morning, we're *all* identical."

I've always appreciated those with enough basic knowledge of middle school science not to ask if they are identical triplets. (Unlike the *Maury* show where guys claim they can't possibly be the baby's father because "We weren't in a relationship.")

But the biggest challenge Lloyd and I faced on our

strolls was trying to block the neighborhood grandmas from the old country who were hell-bent on grabbing, cheek-pinching and most of all-- kissing our children. We could have used a bullhorn.

"Step back from the babies and keep your lips where we can see them! Nothing personal but we have absolutely no idea where those lips have been!"

By the time the kids were six months old, we had offended hundreds of old ladies from dozens of old countries.

When the children were eight months old, we moved from Queens to North Carolina. Suddenly the reactions to the very same three babies were:

"Y'all have got your hands full!" and "What a blessing!" instead of:

"Better you than me." and "I'd kill myself."

Talk about culture shock.

Occasionally the two cultures collided. After one particularly awful sleepless night in our new home, a woman passing us in the supermarket aisle commented predictably:

"What a blessing!" Lloyd looked at me through puffy red slits.

"I swear the next person who says that I'm going to say: 'Yeah, fuck you and your blessing!'"

There's no place like home.

E. Heading South in More Ways than One- A Post-Infantry Roundup

We moved for some very simple reasons: As the babies got bigger and their infant carriers got heavier, the apartment got smaller and the hike up to it took longer.

And oh the sisters and sisters-in-law--woe was they.

How could they help raise their nieces and nephew from so far away?

Wait. Are you the same people who never came over when we lived a half hour away from you?

My start as a southern mom was shaky at best. An extremely perceptive saleswoman at a craft store looked me over and asked:

"You don't scrapbook do you?" (I wanted to answer with: "Since when is 'scrapbook' a verb?")

Then I went to a giant consignment sale held in the building that houses livestock competitions during the state fair. Once I saw the stampede inside, it made total sense. I still refer to this annual event that I never went back to as:

"La Corrida de Mamis". (The Running of the Mommies)

At Five Months My Ass

A few months after we moved, Carly got it together and started sleeping through the night. But Hayley and Jacob took turns waking up and crying at least once a night every single night clear through toddlerhood. More than once I stood in their room and dozed off mid-lullaby. Lloyd and I stumbled through literally *years* of way too much work / way too little sleep. Parents of newborn multiples always ask with desperation in their voice:

"When does it get easier?"

Truth be told, it really didn't get easier for us until

the kids started school. Maybe it's because it forced us into a solid routine or because somebody else was watching them all day. While it was heartrending to see them go, school was a lifeline for Lloyd and me, not to mention for scores of pedestrians in the path of the minivan during my mid-morning nap. Although school probably made life harder for our kids.

Separating Twisty Ties is Trickier than it Looks

When my babies were babies they reminded me of those twisty ties that come with your trash bags:

1. They all came out of the same box.
2. They were virtually interchangeable.
3. We kept them together in one big cluster.
4. I spent a lot of time looking around the kitchen floor to see where they'd gone to.

Once they were school age, since my twisty

ties didn't seem to care either way, we opted to untwist them and put them in different classes so they could have their own experiences as individuals. So much for that. The non-identical girls were still always called by each other's name and all three of them were treated like a novelty act: "The Triplets". ("That's Jacob. He's one of 'The Triplets'.") In addition, having the last name "Fox" didn't help. Throughout elementary school, students and teachers alike would see any or all of them in the hallway and yell out:

"What did the Foxes say?!" which I'm told is a take on a game that only I never heard of. At camp they were accosted with:

"Who let the Foxes out? Who?! Who?!"

Laughing IS Conceivable...And Humor Heals.

You know that special bond all multiple siblings have? So when does that start? You also hear about the secret language they have between them. Well, I'm not sure if it's a secret language but the other day they were playing the board game "Sorry!" and Jacob moved his pawn then got in Hayley's face and renamed the game "That's What You Get, Bitch!"

Laughing *IS* Conceivable No Matter How Many You're Carrying

Afterword: **The Fox Kids- Where Are They Now?** (How should I know? They're probably around here somewhere.)

If my kids are any indication, a child's personality is fully developed in the womb and never changes much.

Jacob was always easy to find in utero. He implanted himself in one spot and never once budged in thirty-four weeks. If a doctor hadn't reached in and grabbed him, I'd have a seventy-two pound seventh grader lying there now. It was such a positive experience for him, he stages a reenactment every weekend on the couch.

Carly, if you recall, started out in the pregnancy as "Triplet C" but ultimately became "Triplet B" by pushing her sister out of the way. In the twelve years or so since that triumph, she's had her sights on the "Triplet A" spot. If one of her siblings runs home waving a paper:

"Look! I got 100 on my test!" she'll be right behind them flaunting hers.

"I got 100 also! But I answered the extra credit question so it's really 102!"

While common nicknames for "Carly" might be "Carl" or "Carlita" we found a more appropriate one for ours: "Wendy One-Up".

Hayley was the womb instigator. During most

nights of the pregnancy, Lloyd and I and the three babies would all be asleep. Then all of a sudden, in the wee hours, Hayley would kick Carly who would kick Jacob who would kick Hayley who would kick Carly who would kick Jacob who would kick Hayley who would kick Carly who would kick Jacob who would kick Hayley who would kick Carly who would kick Jacob who would kick Hayley. Now that they are twelve and external, things are much better. Hayley turns on the TV and ignores it while she plays a game on her tablet. Then the other two come in and change the channel because she's not watching it. Then Hayley kicks Carly who kicks Jacob who kicks Hayley who kicks Carly who kicks Jacob who kicks Hayley who kicks Carly who kicks Jacob who kicks Hayley who kicks Carly who kicks Jacob who kicks Hayley and I, out of force of habit or conditioned response, get up to pee. And Lloyd, forever being the loving, supportive husband, he goes too.

Come Learn from My Confusion: Questions That Still Stump Me

Embarrassing as it is to admit being a former stand-up comic, there are questions that I've gotten over and over for more than a decade to which I still have no good comeback.

1) ***"Did you have them naturally?"*** (First, let me thank you from the bottom of my body part for not mentioning it.)

Besides that I find the question a mite personal, I find it confusing. I always feel the need to clarify as I answer.

"Do you mean did they go in naturally or did they come out naturally? Well, either way, no they didn't."

2) *"Are they twins?"*

I've gotten this a lot because Carly and Hayley have always been about the same size while Jacob has always been slightly taller. When we're all together it's easy enough to say:

"Actually, they're triplets."

But when I have just the girls with me and people ask if they're twins… "Uh, uh…"

I usually end up saying:

"That's sort of a trick question. They're triplets. I have a son too." (I tack on that last part so their head won't explode figuring out how two kids can be triplets.) It's not perfect but probably better than:

"No. They're 2/3 of triplets" which makes them sound like the larger part of one chunky kid.

3) *"Do triplets run in your family?"*

This is a total puzzler. Twins? Sure. But do *triplets* run in *anybody's* family? Carly has volunteered to field this one from now on. The next time somebody asks:

"Triplets? Do they run in your family?" she'll chime in with:

"Yes it does run in our family. I'm a triplet. My sister is a triplet. And so is my brother."

4) *"You didn't do that IVF stuff did you?"*

If they or someone close to them has fertility issues, I'm more than willing to share. But posed like this? I can almost see their list of moral evils where IVF ranks halfway between voting and voodoo. I'm always dying to say:

"In fact, I did. On Tuesdays I play bingo. On Thursdays I play God."

I usually just walk away. I really have no interest in talking to this person.

5) *What's it like having triplets?*

Since I have no other parenting experience to compare it to, it's kind of like asking me what it's like to be a 5'2 1/4" Jewish woman. Uh... "Fine I guess?"

Come Learn from My Blunders: My Final Two Cents to Parents of Many Babies...or Even Just One

1) Always bring a list of questions with you to the doctor and actually ask them.

If you don't write 'em, you forget to ask 'em. If you forget to ask 'em, you spend all night hallucinating the worst possible scenario answers and being pissed at yourself for not asking.

2) Don't be a hero. Whether you're pregnant or already had him, her, or them, take help from anyone trustworthy / normal who's willing to give it.

3) Forgive and move on. Don't waste precious time and energy whining about people who should be there to help but aren't. (Says the woman who spent twelve years and twelve pages kvetching about it.) Trust me. Rehashing will only keep you from your own peace and not make them one bit less useless.

4) Completely ignore online support group people who think all you need is a pep talk.

"You can do it! You're stronger than you think! I have six kids under two and I do it! So can you! You've got this!"

Aw shut the… I'm all for cheerleading but sometimes you need real medical intervention, emotional support, and physical assistance and less rah rah sis boom bah.

(If you are even considering harming yourself or your baby/babies, call 911 immediately. If you suspect you may be suffering from postpartum depression, call your doctor right away, visit Postpartum Progress at: http://postpartumprogress.com and/or contact Postpartum Support International (PSI) at www.postpartum.net, support@postpartum.net, or 1-800-944-4773)*

5) Even if you've tried for years to have kids, you're still allowed to regret having them occasionally.

For the first several overwhelming, bleary-eyed months, I referred to this whole baby thing as "a mistake" and even though I've always adored my kids, back then, it sure felt like I meant it.

(Again: If you are even considering harming yourself or your baby/babies, call 911 immediately. For postpartum depression, call your doctor right away, visit Postpartum Progress at: http://postpartumprogress.com and/or contact Postpartum Support International (PSI) at www.postpartum.net, support@postpartum.net, or 1-800-944-4773)*

*Information is provided as a reference to readers and is not an endorsement of any company or organization. The author has had no direct personal experience with either organization listed above.

6) Keep in mind that nobody can read yours.

"They know what I'm going through. I shouldn't have to tell them that I need help!"

You're right. They probably do and you probably shouldn't. But sometimes to get the assistance you need, you have to put anger and resentment aside and calmly, clearly and repeatedly tell family, friends, -- even partners:

"Look I'm drowning here. Could you please do some laundry or watch the babies so I can take a shower and eat?"

Now there is no doubt that they know what they should know.

7) Take care of yourself first no matter what.

I know. The babies have to be fed and changed and comforted and you can't do any of it if you're face down on the floor dead from exhaustion, starvation, and the stink of your own body odor. The best advice came from Lloyd's friend Allan:

"Before you do anything for the kids, make sure you eat and go to the bathroom."

Granted, I've occasionally combined the two to save time but this is advice I still adhere to today.

And if you think raising triplets is a lot of work, can you imagine doing it while having another full-time job? Or while being dead broke? Well, I didn't have to imagine either. Coming soon:

Laughing *IS* Conceivable: Even When You Have a Dead-End Job--Or 23

Laughing *IS* Conceivable: Even When the Poverty Line is Just a Pipedream

About the Author

Lori Shandle-Fox's humor and non-humor bits and pieces have appeared in: <u>The Washington Post</u>, <u>The Philadelphia Inquirer</u>, <u>Carolina Woman</u>, <u>Newsday</u>, <u>Lilith Magazine</u> and <u>Reader's Digest</u> and on NPR and GrokNation.com. Her Laughing *IS* Conceivable book series, blog, and podcast are designed to de-stress people from life's anxieties big and small- all stressful times that she herself has experienced.

Lori is a native New Yorker currently living in North Carolina. She and her husband Lloyd remain committed fans of their New York sports teams. (For better or worse, till death do they part.)

www.ingramcontent.com/pod-product-compliance
Lightning Source LLC
Chambersburg PA
CBHW050555300426
44112CB00013B/1923